COVER: "THE COWBOY"

SHOWS US THE ROUGH COUNTRY OF THE WESTERN RANGES. THE WORKING MEN OF THE EARLY WEST RESPECTED THEIR HARSH LAND ALTHOUGH IT REQUIRED ALL THEIR SKILLS TO COMPLETE A DAY'S WORK.

FREDERIC REMINGTON UNDERSTOOD THIS COUNTRY, ITS RUGGEDNESS AND ITS BEAUTY. HE FELT ITS CHALLENGES AS DID THE BOLD MEN WHO LIVED AND WORKED UPON IT. HE KNEW THE HORSEMEN, THE HORSE AND THE SADDLE AND PAINTED THEM IN EXCITING AND REALISTIC DETAIL.

IN THIS PICTURE, WITH HOOVES FLYING, THE BRONCO MUST PICK HIS WAY CAREFULLY BETWEEN GIANT BOULDERS AND SHARP ROCKS. WE ALMOST BRACE OUR FEET IN THE STIRRUPS WITH THE STRAINING COWBOY AS HE PLUNGES DOWN THE HILL.

COURRIERS

THE CHEYENNE   THOMAS GILCREASE INSTITUTE, TULSA, OKLAHOMA

DEDICATED TO CARL S. DENTZEL, FRIEND, AND DIRECTOR
OF THE SOUTHWEST MUSEUM IN LOS ANGELES

SPECIAL THANKS TO THE REMINGTON ART MEMORIAL MUSEUM,
OGDENSBURG, NEW YORK

LIBRARY OF CONGRESS CATALOGING-IN-PUBLICATION DATA
RABOFF, ERNEST LLOYD.
     FREDERIC REMINGTON.
     (ART FOR CHILDREN)
REPRINT. ORIGINALLY PUBLISHED: GARDEN CITY, N.Y.: DOUBLEDAY, 1973. SUMMARY: A BRIEF BIOGRAPHY OF FREDERIC REMINGTON ACCOMPANIES
FIFTEEN COLOR REPRODUCTIONS AND CRITICAL INTERPRETATIONS OF HIS WORKS. 1. REMINGTON, FREDERIC, 1861-1909 –JUVENILE LITERATURE. 2. ARTISTS–
UNITED STATES – BIOGRAPHY–JUVENILE LITERATURE. 3. REMINGTON, FREDERIC, 1861-1909 – CRITICISM AND INTERPRETATION–JUVENILE LITERATURE. 4. WEST (U.S.)
IN ART – JUVENILE LITERATURE. [1. REMINGTON, FREDERIC, 1861-1909. 2. ARTISTS. 3. WEST (U.S.) IN ART. 4. ART APPRECIATION] I. REMINGTON, FREDERIC, 1861-1909.
II. TITLE. III. SERIES: ART FOR CHILDREN.
ND537.R4R3   1988   759.13   [92]   87-16865   ISBN 0-397-32220-8
     "A HARPER TROPHY BOOK"   ISBN 0-06-446079-7 (PBK.)   87-17698

FREDERIC REMINGTON

By Ernest Raboff

ART
FOR
CHILDREN

A HARPER TROPHY BOOK

HARPER & ROW, PUBLISHERS

FREDERIC REMINGTON

WAS BORN IN CANTON, NEW YORK ON OCTOBER 1, 1861. HIS MOTHER, CLARA SACKRIDER MARRIED SETH PIERREPONT REMINGTON WHO WAS FIRST A CAVALRY OFFICER AND LATER A NEWSPAPER PUBLISHER. FREDERIC WAS A FINE ATHLETE AS A BOY AND SPENT MUCH TIME SWIMMING, FISHING AND RIDING HORSES. HE ALSO DREW PICTURES AND HIS FAVORITE SUBJECTS WERE HORSES, SOLDIERS AND INDIANS.

AFTER TWO YEARS IN A MILITARY ACADEMY, REMINGTON ATTENDED ART SCHOOL AT YALE UNIVERSITY. DURING HIS TWO YEARS THERE HE WON FAME AS A FOOTBALL PLAYER RATHER THAN AS A STUDENT.

LEAVING COLLEGE AT AGE NINETEEN, HE HEADED WEST AND SPENT OVER FOUR YEARS AS A COWBOY, A WAGON TRAIN HAND AND A RANCHER. HE SKETCHED EVERYTHING HE SAW WHEREVER HE ROAMED, FROM THE WYOMING BADLANDS TO THE ROCKY MOUNTAINS, T THE ARIZONA DESERT AND THE TEXAS PLAINS, RECORDING IN VIVID PICTURES THE ROUGH LIFE OF THE FRONTIER TOWNS.

RETURNING TO NEW YORK, HE MARRIED EVA CATEN, BUT HE CONTINUED TO VISIT HIS FAVORED FAR WEST, MEXICO OR CANADA EVERY YEAR.

HIS ART MADE HIM FAMOUS BY THE AGE OF THIRTY. IN HIS TWENTY-THREE YEARS AS AN ARTIST, REMINGTON CREATED 2739 DRAWINGS AND PAINTINGS, 25 BRONZE SCULPTURES AND WROTE 8 BOOKS.

THE ARTIST DIED ON CHRISTMAS DAY, 1909, AT THE AGE OF FORTY-EIGHT.

PORTRAIT OF THE ARTIST BY ERNEST RABOFF

FREDERIC REMINGTON's

WORK AS AN ILLUSTRATOR, PAINTER AND SCULPTOR COMBINED REALISM WITH STORYTELLING. HE GAVE US AN OBJECTIVE VIEW OF AMERICA'S WESTERN FRONTIER AND CHRONICLED ITS GROWTH WITH A RIPENING TALENT.

OWEN WISTER WROTE: "FREDERIC REMINGTON IS NOT MERELY AN ARTIST; HE IS A NATIONAL TREASURE." HE HAS PICTURED THE AMERICAN INDIAN AS NO ONE ELSE AND HAS TOLD OF HIS GRANDEUR AND HIS TRAGEDY COMPLETELY.

ROYAL CORTISSOZ WROTE THAT REMINGTON "GOT INTO A WAY OF DRAWING SKILFULLY [sic] AND CLEVERLY, SO THAT HE PUT HIS SUBJECT ACCURATELY BEFORE YOU AND MADE YOU FEEL ITS SPECIAL TANG.

"HIS SUCCESS WAS DUE NOT ONLY TO MANUAL DEXTERITY BUT TO HIS WHOLE-HEARTED RESPONSE TO THE STRAIGHT FORWARD, MANLY CHARM OF THE LIFE WHICH BY INSTINCT HE KNEW HOW TO SHARE."

CORTISSOZ FURTHER WROTE: "IT ALL MAKES AN EXHILARATING SPECTACLE, AND THESE PICTURES ARE FILLED BESIDES WITH KEEN, DRY AIR AND DAZZLING LIGHT. THE JOY OF LIVING GETS INTO FREDERIC REMINGTON'S WORK."

MOUNTAIN MAN,
THOMAS GILCREASE INSTITUTE OF AMERICAN HISTORY AND ART.

"THE MYSTERY OF THE BUFFALO GUN" SHOWS A BAND OF INDIANS AND THEIR HORSES STARTLED BY THE ROAR OF A WHITE MAN'S RIFLE.

ALTHOUGH REMINGTON AND OTHERS OF HIS TIME REFERRED TO THESE BEASTS AS BUFFALOES THEY ACTUALLY ARE BISON. BUFFALOES INHABIT A FEW WARM REGIONS OF ASIA AND AFRICA. THEY HAVE LONGER HORNS, SHORTER HAIR AND NO HUMPS ON THEIR BACKS.

FOR THE INDIANS, THIS PLENTIFUL RANGE ANIMAL WAS A MEANS OF LIFE. FOOD, CLOTHING AND TOOLS CAME FROM THE BISON. TENTS BOATS, BEDDING, ROPES, SADDLE BAGS AND BOWSTRINGS WERE MADE FROM ITS HIDE. ITS HORNS BECAME SPOONS. COLORFUL CEREMONIAL MASKS FOR SACRED DANCES WERE DECORATED WITH HORN AND IT WAS USED AS A SIGN OF DISTINCTION ON BRAVE INDIANS' WAR BONNETS.

BY THE 1820s, BUFFALO HUNTING FOR PROFIT HAD BEGUN. YET, IN 1850, HERDS TOTALED 20,000,000 AND OFTEN BLOCKED THE PASSAGE OF RAILROAD TRAINS. FORTY YEARS LATER, THEY NUMBERED ONLY 551.

THIS PAINTING OWN MYSTER IS THAT, WITHOUT A BISON IN SIGHT, IT PORTRAYS THE END OF ITS REIGN OVER THE WEST.

HER CALF

REMINGTON ART MEMORIAL MUSEUM, OGDENSBURG

THE MYSTERY OF THE BUFFALO GUN

"THE UNKNOWN EXPLORERS" WAS ONE OF TEN WORKS REMINGTON PAINTED IN A "GREAT EXPLORERS" SERIES FOR COLLIER'S WEEKLY MAGAZINE IN 1905-1906.

IN THIS PAINTING, HE SHOWS CABEZA DE VACA, THE SPANISH EXPLORER OF NORTH AND SOUTH AMERICA, WHO SPENT EIGHT YEARS WALKING FROM A SHIPWRECK ON THE COAST OF TEXAS TO MEXICO CITY IN 1536. HIS REPORTS OF GREAT TREASURES IN THESE LANDS LED FRANCISCO CORONADO TO SEEK THE SEVEN CITIES OF CIBOLA AND GRAN QUIVIRA. HE DISCOVERED INSTEAD THE JAGGED CONTINENTAL DIVIDE IN THE ROCKY MOUNTAINS AND HIS FOLLOWERS FOUND THE COLORFUL GRAND CANYON AND THE COLORADO RIVER. FROM THESE EXPLORERS ALSO, THE INDIANS ACQUIRED HORSES FOR THE FIRST TIME AND THEREBY CHANGED THE HISTORY OF THE WEST.

REMINGTON'S PORTRAIT SERIES INCLUDED THE FRENCHMEN, RADISSON, GROSEILLIERS AND DE LA VERENDRYE; THE SCOTSMAN, MACKENZIE; THE SPANIARDS, DE SOTO, DE VACA AND CORONADO; AND THE AMERICANS, CLARK, LEWIS, JEDEDIAH SMITH AND ZEBULON PIKE. BUT IT WAS FOR THE HUNDREDS OF UNKNOWN EXPLORERS THAT FREDERIC REMINGTON HELD THE HIGHEST RESPECT.

AMERICAN, MEXICAN AND FRENCH PIONEER TYPES

UNKNOWN EXPLORERS

THE UNKNOWN EXPLORERS (DETAIL)   REMINGTON ART MEMORIAL MUSEUM, OGDENSBURG

"MACKENZIE", THE SCOTTISH EXPLORER OF NORTH AMERICA, WAS GREATLY ADMIRED BY ARTIST-WRITER REMINGTON NOT ONLY FOR HIS COURAGE BUT FOR HIS INTELLIGENCE AND EDUCATION AS WELL.

FRONTIERSMEN

REMINGTON ART MEMORIAL MUSEUM, OGDENSBURG, N.Y.

HERE THE ARTIST SHOWS MACKENZIE IN SEARCH OF AN INLAND WATER WAY TO THE PACIFIC OCEAN. BEGINNING IN NORTHWEST CANADA, HE WAS DISAPPOINTED 1120 MILES LATER WHEN THE JOURNEY LED HIM INSTEAD TO THE ARCTIC OCEAN. HE NAMED THE WATERWAY THE RIVER OF DISAPPOINTMENT. IT WAS LATER CHANGED TO THE MACKENZIE RIVER.

IN HIS BROAD-BRIMMED HAT AND FULL-LENGTH CAPE, ALEXANDER MACKE STANDS WATCHFULLY IN MID-BOAT. IN THE PROW OF THE BOAT, AN INDIA GUIDE HOLDS A LONG POLE TO PUSH THEM AWAY FROM ROCKS IN THE WATE HIS RIGHT ARM ACTS AS A SIGNAL TO THE RUDDER-MAN WHO STEERS BEHIND THE EIGHT MEN PADDLING WITH MATCHED STROKES.

ONE SIDE OF THE BARREN ROCK CANYON IS COVERED BY AN AFTER NOON'S PURPLE SHADOW. THE WISE EXPLORER AND HIS TEN MEN KNOW THEY MUST END THEIR DAY'S VOYAGE BEFORE DARKNESS BEGIN

MACKENZIE

"THE EPISODE OF THE BUFFALO HUNT" IS A PAINTING CHARGED WITH DRAMATIC AND BREATHTAKING EXCITEMENT. ACTION AND DANGER BURST FROM THE CENTER.

A RACING BISON, WITH MASSIVE HEAD LOWERED, TURNS AND REARS, LIFTING THE GASPING HORSE COMPLETELY OFF THE GROUND AND TOSSING THE RIDER HIGH INTO THE DUSTY AIR.

TAKEN BY SURPRISE, THE INDIAN HUNTER HOLDS HIS BOW IN ONE HAND WHILE HIS PACK OF ARROWS STRAINS FROM ITS FEATHERED THONGS BEHIND HIM.

HUNTING BISON WAS EVEN MORE DANGEROUS BEFORE THE INDIANS RODE HORSES. ON FOOT, THEY HAD TO APPROACH THE ANIMAL WITHIN A FEW FEET SO AS TO DOWN HIM WITH THE FIRST WELL-DIRECTED ARROW.

INDIAN WITH HIS HORSE   REMINGTON ART MEMORIAL MUSEUM, OGDENSBURG

AS AN ATHLETE HIMSELF, FREDERIC REMINGTON UNDERSTOOD AND ADMIRED THE COURAGE OF THE INDIAN HUNTERS AND THEIR WELL-TRAINED HORSES.

THE EPISODE OF THE BUFFALO HUNT

"BRINGING HOME THE NEW COOK" PORTRAYS AN IMPORTANT EVENT IN THE LIVES OF COWBOYS. FOOD AND ITS PREPARATION MEANT A GREAT DEAL TO THESE HARDY MEN WHO WORKED THROUGH RAIN, SNOW, WINDS AND DUST STORMS. LONG HOURS RIDING, WRESTLING STEERS, DRIVING HERDS AND PROTECTING THEM FROM HARM, MADE MEALTIMES ONE OF THEIR FEW REAL PLEASURES.

COOKING FOR COWBOYS WAS A DEMANDING ROLE. THE COOK WHO FAILED TO SATISFY THEIR TASTES OR THEIR STOMACHS WAS SOON SENT OUT TO RIDE RANGE OR TO FIND A NEW CAMP IN WHICH TO SHOW HIS SKILL

THE COWBOYS, AS REMINGTON RECORDS HERE, WERE ALWAYS READY TO GIVE THE NEW COOK A LOUD AND ROUSING WELCOME. WITH HAND GUNS BLASTING THE AIR AND URGING THE HORSES ONWARD, THE UNRESTRAINED RIDERS SHOW THEIR EAGERNESS TO TASTE THEIR NEXT CAMP MEAL.

THE MIDDAY MEAL

REMINGTON ART MEMORIAL MUSEUM, OGDENSBURG, N.Y.

BRINGING HOME THE NEW COOK

"HAULING IN THE GILL NET" IS AN EXAMPLE OF FREDERIC REMINGTON'S INTEREST IN THE MEN WHO CHALLENGED MOUNTAINS, FORESTS, DESERTS, PRAIRIES AND WATER IN ALL KINDS OF WEATHER. HE DREW, PAINTED, SCULPTED, WROTE AND WORKED WITH THESE MEN WHO NEEDED TO USE BOTH THEIR MINDS AND THEIR MUSCLES TO EARN THEIR DAILY FOOD. THE ARTIST RECORDED FACTS ABOUT THEM SO ALL OF US COULD UNDERSTAND THEIR COURAGE AND INTELLIGENCE.

HER FIRST MUSKIE

REMINGTON ART MEMORIAL MUSEUM, OGDENSBURG

REMINGTON'S FISHERMEN IN THEIR BARK CANOE, LONG AND NARROW, FRAGILE AND DELICATELY BALANCED, STRUGGLE AGAINST THE WHITE CAPPED WAVES AND THE CHILL WINDS THAT BLOW THROUGH THEIR HAIR. THEY KEEP THEIR LEFT SHIRT SLEEVES ROLLED UP, READY TO PLUNGE THEIR ARMS DOWN TO THE NET IN THE COLD WATER WHEN IT IS NECESSARY. THE MAN IN THE BACK OF THE BOAT BALANCES CAREFULLY, MAKING AS LITTLE MOTION AS POSSIBLE WITH HIS PADDLE.

WE CAN CLEARLY SENSE THE PHYSICAL STRENGTH REQUIRED TO PADDLE A FRAIL CANOE IN SUCH CHOPPY WATER, TO HAUL UP THE WATER-SOAKED NET HEAVY WITH FISH AND TO KEEP FROM TIPPING THE SHALLOW CRAFT INTO THE WATER.

THESE EXPERIENCED MEN WERE ABLE TO SUCCEED IN A HARSH ENVIRONMENT.

HAULING IN THE GILL NET   REMINGTON ART MEMORIAL MUSEUM, OGDENSBURG

"BRONCO BUSTER"

WAS BEGUN IN 1895. THE BRONZE WAS CAST ON REMINGTON'S 34TH BIRTHDAY, OCTOBER FIRST. MORE CASTINGS WERE MADE OF THIS PIECE, HIS FIRST SCULPTURE, THAN OF ANY OF HIS OTHERS.

FREDERIC REMINGTON HAD NO FORMAL TRAINING AS A SCULPTOR AND PROBABLY INVENTED HIS OWN CREATIVE TECHNIQUES. RICARDO BERTELLI OF THE ROMAN BRONZE WORKS WAS A SKILLED CRAFTSMAN WHOSE CARE ASSURED HIGH QUALITY IN REMINGTON'S BRONZE WORK. THE TWO MEN WERE GOOD FRIENDS AND OFTEN WORKED TOGETHER IN THE FOUNDRY CASTING MANY OF THE ARTIST'S FINE SCULPTURES.

REMINGTON'S LOVE OF HORSES DATED FROM HIS CHILDHOOD YEARS. HIS DRAWINGS AND HIS SKILL AS A RIDER WON HIM FRIENDS IN THE WEST WHERE A COWBOY OFTEN HAD SIX TO EIGHT HORSES.

HE REQUESTED HIS EPITAPH TO READ: HE KNEW THE HORSE.

MEXICAN VAQUEROS BREAKING A BRONC

REMINGTON ART MEMORIAL MUSEUM, OGDENSBURG

THE BRONCO BUSTER   REMINGTON ART MEMORIAL MUSEUM, OGDENSBURG

"COMING THROUGH THE RYE" IS AN
EXTRAORDINARY PIECE OF SCULPTURE WITH SO MUCH EXCITEMENT THAT
IT IS FUN TO FIRST LET ONE'S EYES ROAM WHEREVER THEY WILL.

IN STUDYING THIS MASTERPIECE, WE NOTICE THAT EACH HORSE'S
HEAD IS HELD IN A DIFFERENT POSITION. EACH SHOWS THE LABOR
OF GALLOPING

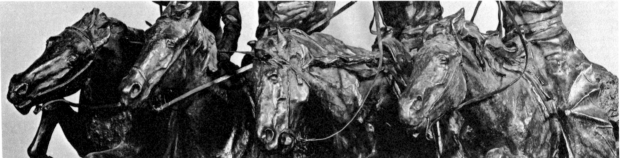

BY ITS STRAINING EYES AND FLARING NOSTRILS. NOTICE REMINGTON
SKILL IN RECORDING THE POWERFUL MOTIONS OF THE HORSES' LEGS.

ABOVE THE HORSES, WE SEE THAT THE POSITIONS OF THEIR HEADS
ARE ALMOST DUPLICATED BY THE HEADS OF THEIR REVELING RIDERS
THE SCULPTOR IS SHOWING US THE HARMONY OF THE HORSE WITH
THE MAN. THEY SEEM TO BE FOUR UNITS OF SINGLE MOTION.

THE COWBOY'S LIFE OFTEN DEPENDED ON HIS PONY AS MUCH AS
ON HIS OWN ARMS AND LEGS.

FREDERIC REMINGTON WAS AN ARTIST-HISTORIAN. NO DETAIL
ESCAPED HIS ARTISTIC ATTENTION. HATS, KERCHIEFS, SHIRTS,
GAUNTLET GLOVES, PISTOLS, TOSSED REINS, TROUSERS, CHAPS,
BOOTS AND STIRRUPS ARE MASTERFULLY CAST FOR A RECORD
OF THE WEST.

COMING THROUGH THE RYE   REMINGTON ART MEMORIAL MUSEUM, OGDENSBURG

"THE SANTA FE TRADE" BEGAN IN THE EARLY 1800's ALONG THE SANTA FE TRAIL. THE 780 MILE TRAIL ORIGINATED IN INDEPENDENCE, MISSOURI, AND ENDED IN SANTA FE, NEW MEXICO. IT WAS ONE OF THE LONGEST COMMERCIAL ROUTES IN THE EARLY UNITED STATES.

THE EARLIEST TRAVELLERS CARRIED THEIR GOODS ON PACK HORSES. IN 1821, WILLIAM BECKNELL LED THE FIRST WAGONS ACROSS THE ROUTE. A PROFITABLE TRADE WAS BEGUN. MANUFACTURED GOODS FROM THE EASTERN STATES WERE EXCHANGED FOR FURS, MULES, GOLD AND SILVER IN SANTA FE. CARAVANS WERE ESCORTED AT TIMES BY THE U.S. CAVALRY TO HELP PROTECT THEM FROM HOSTILE INDIANS AND MEXICAN BANDITS.

ABOUT 80 WAGONS AND 150 MEN CARRIED GOODS VALUED AT $130,000 ALONG THE BUSY TRAIL EACH YEAR. REMINGTON PAINTED THIS TYPICAL SCENE BEFORE THE OPENING OF THE RAILROAD WHICH ENDED THE SANTA FE TRADE AFTER ONLY 23 YEARS.

IN LESS THAN 90 YEARS, FROM THE LEWIS AND CLARK EXPEDITION

IN 1804 TO THE LAST INDIAN WAR AGAINST THE SIOUX AT PINE RIDGE, SOUTH DAKOTA, IN 1891 THE

WILD WEST

WAS GONE FOREVER.

INTERIOR MOUNTAIN CABIN   REMINGTON MEMORIAL ART MUSEUM, OGDENSBURG

THE SANTA FE TRADE

REMINGTON ART MEMORIAL MUSEUM, OGDENSBURG

"HIS FIRST LESSON"

WAS AS HARD ON THE COWBOY AS IT WAS ON THE HORSE.

BREAKING A HORSE TO WEARING A SADDLE AND CARRYING A RIDER ON ITS PREVIOUSLY BARE BACK WAS A TOUGH DAILY CHORE AND A NECESSITY FOR THE COWBOYS.

TO GET MOUNTED IN THE SADDLE WITHOUT GETTING A KICK FROM A FLYING HOOF WAS ONLY THE FIRST TRIAL FOR THE WARY RIDER. ONCE SEATED HE DOES NOT REMAIN STILL. THE BRONCO TAKES OFF LIKE AN EXPLODING FIRECRACKER, BOUNCING ACROSS THE GROUND, FLEXING HIS ARCHED BACK IN TERRIFYING LEAPS AND REARING ON OUTSTRETCHED HIND LEGS.

TRYING TO THROW OFF THE UNWELCOME COWBOY, THE UNTAMED ANIMAL LANDS ON HIS STRONG FRONT LEGS WHILE THRUSTING HIS REAR ONES BACK AND UP TOWARD THE SKY.

THEN A LONG RUN BY THE DETERMINED HORSE IN A NEW ATTEMPT FOR FREEDOM FROM THE RIDER, A FINAL SERIES OF BUCKS AND THE FIRST LESSON IS OVER.

SOON, A MUTUAL RESPECT BINDS ANIMAL AND MAN INTO AN ALMOST INSEPARABLE WORKING TEAM.

Barracks at Calgary —
Frederic Remington

BARRACKS AT CALGARY

HIS FIRST LESSON

AMON CARTER MUSEUM / FORT WORTH

MAKING THE SNOWSHOE   REMINGTON MEMORIAL ART MUSEUM, OGDENSBURG

"APACHES LISTENING" IS A QUIET PAINTING OF A SMALL BAND OF NOMADIC INDIANS WHO ROAMED THE DESERTS, CANYONS AND ROCKY MOUNTAINS OF THE SOUTHWEST UNITED STATES.

IN THE FRONT OF THE PICTURE, A MOUNTAIN'S BLUE SHADOW FALLS ACROSS THE GREAT OPEN LAND. WE ALMOST STAND BESIDE THE ARTIST AND FEEL THE SILENCE WHICH FREDERIC REMINGTON CAPTURES.

HORSES AND MEN ARE STILL. NOTHING MOVES. THE ONLY SIGN OF ACTION IS IN THE LEADER'S SILENTLY RAISED ARM, POINTING A DIRECTION FOR HIS COMPANIONS' ATTENTION.

WE CAN SEE THAT THE DAY IS NEAR NOON. PALE SHADOWS FALL DIRECTLY UNDER THE RIDERS PAUSING IN THE SUNLIGHT AND BLUE PATCHES REST ON THE TIPS OF THE DISTANT MOUNTAIN RANGE ACROSS THE FLAT, DRY DESERT.

MEN WHO LIVE IN OPEN COUNTRY WHERE THERE ARE FEW PEOPLE SOON LEARN THE VALUE OF SILENCE AND LISTENING.

INDIAN PONY   REMINGTON MEMORIAL ART MUSEUM, OGDENSBURG

APACHES LISTENING

'THE STAMPEDE' WAS THE LAST SCULPTURE CREATED BY FREDERIC REMINGTON.

COMBINING A WELL-TRAINED EYE FOR ACCURATE DETAIL WITH HIS LOVE FOR THE WEST, THIS MASTERFUL WORK WAS COMPLETED IN 1909 JUST BEFORE HIS DEATH. IT IS A DRAFTSMAN'S FINAL TRIBUTE TO THE ALMOST FRATERNAL BOND SHARED WITH THE COWBOYS, THE RANGE ANIMALS AND THEIR LIVES.

THEODORE ROOSEVELT, WHO GREATLY ADMIRED FREDERIC REMINGTON, WROTE IN 1910: " THE INDIAN IS CIVILIZED, THE COWBOY IS PASSING, THE RANGE CATTLE ARE TAMING, EVEN THE CAYUSE (INDIAN PONY) IS PASSING INTO HISTORY. ONE MAN'S WORK, HOWEVER, WILL PRESERVE THEM FOR ALL TIME IN PICTURES AND IN BRONZE....
THIS MAN WAS REMINGTON..."

BRONCOS AND TIMBER WOLVES   REMINGTON ART MEMORIAL MUSEUM, OGDENSBURG

THE STAMPEDE

THOMAS GILCREASE INSTITUTE, TULSA, OKLAHOMA

THE TWILIGHT OF THE INDIAN   REMINGTON ART MEMORIAL MUSEUM ,OGDENSBURG